Snap books®

Zodiac Fun

Gemini, Libra, and Aquarius

All about the AIR Signs

by Jen Jones

CAPSTONE PRESS
a capstone imprint

Snap Books are published by Capstone Press,
151 Good Counsel Drive, P.O. Box 669, Mankato, Minnesota 56002.
www.capstonepress.com

092009
005618CGS10

Books published by Capstone Press are manufactured with paper
containing at least 10 percent post-consumer waste.

Library of Congress Cataloging-in-Publication Data
Jones, Jen.
    Gemini, Libra, and Aquarius : all about the air signs / by Jen Jones.
    p. cm. — (Snap. Zodiac fun)
    Summary: "Provides information about the air signs of the zodiac" — Provided by publisher.
    Includes bibliographical references and index.
    ISBN 978-1-4296-4012-1 (library binding)
    1. Air signs (Astrology) — Juvenile literature. I. Title. II. Series.
BF1727.9.A37J66 2010
133.5'2 — dc22   2009029191

Editor: Katy Kudela   **Designer:** Juliette Peters
Media Researcher: Jo Miller   **Production Specialist:** Laura Manthe

Photo Credits:
Dreamstime/Amineimo, 10 (top left); Getty Images Inc./Carlos Alvarez, 20; Getty Images Inc./WireImage/Jeffrey Mayer,
13; Getty Images Inc./WireImage/John Shearer, 27; iStockphoto/Barbara Sauder, 17 (top left); iStockphoto/Leonid
Nyshko, 10 (top right); NASA/Johns Hopkins University Applied Physics Laboratory/Carnegie Institution of Washington,
9 (bottom left); NASA/JPL, 16 (bottom left), 23 (bottom left); Shutterstock/Aleksandra Nadeina, 5; Shutterstock/
Baloncici, 4 (top left); Shutterstock/Brendan Howard, 12; Shutterstock/Cihan Demirok, 21 (bottom); Shutterstock/Derek
Gordon, 23 (top); Shutterstock/ Durden Images, 6; Shutterstock/ELEN, 24 (top left); Shutterstock/giangrande alessia, 17
(middle); Shutterstock/Ivan Cholakov Gostock-dot-net, 11; Shutterstock/Jan Martin Will, 26; Shutterstock/Joggie Botma,
22; Shutterstock/Karkas, 17 (top right); Shutterstock/Kenneth Sponsler, 9 (top); Shutterstock/Kim Ruoff, 23 (bottom
right); Shutterstock/Kiselev Andrey Valerevich, 24 (bottom); Shutterstock/kristian sekulic, 18; Shutterstock/KULISH
VIKTORIIA, 10 (bottom); Shutterstock/Loskutnikov, 17 (bottom); Shutterstock/Morten Normann Almeland, 9 (bottom
right); Shutterstock/Oxana Zuboff, 15; Shutterstock/ pdesign, 7 (bottom), 14 (bottom); Shutterstock/Sebastian Kaulitzki,
16 (top); Shutterstock/Sebastien Burel, 25; Shutterstock/Simone van den Berg, 16 (bottom right); Shutterstock/terekhov
igor, 24 (top right); Shutterstock/ulisse, 7 (top), 14 (top), 21 (top); Shutterstock/yuri_k, 8; Shutterstock/ZTS, 19

Design Elements
Shutterstock/argus; Shutterstock/Cihan Demirok; Shutterstock/Epic Stock; Shutterstock/Louisanne;
Shutterstock/Mikhail; Shutterstock/pdesign; Shutterstock/Rashevska Nataliia; Shutterstock/sabri deniz kizil;
Shutterstock/solos

Essential content terms are `bold` and are defined at the bottom of the page where they first appear.

Table of Contents

J
133.5
JON

Cracking the Code

Look up at the night sky. Stars are twinkling right before your eyes. Did you know that those stars say something about you? In **astrology**, people track the placement of the stars, sun, moon, and planets to predict a person's future. Just as there are 12 months of the year, there are 12 zodiac signs. People believe these signs say a lot about a person's personality and destiny.

Is astrology for real? Well, plenty of people have doubts. How can millions of people share the same horoscope? The real deal is that astrology is very complicated. Every person has a special chart. Horoscopes simply help explain the personality **traits** of people born under the same sign. On any given day, a horoscope might sound just like you. Or you might think it is way off the chart. And that's OK. Astrology isn't an exact science. Yet learning about it is fun and can even be like cracking a secret code. So put on your detective hat and get ready to learn more about yourself and those around you.

astrology — the study of how the positions of stars and planets affect people's lives

trait — a characteristic that makes a person stand out from others

A Closer Look at Astrology

In astrology, the elements of air, earth, fire, and water act as an umbrella over the 12 signs. Each element has three signs that share like traits. Gemini, Libra, and Aquarius make up the air signs. These signs are like a breath of fresh air. Bursting with ideas, these signs are sharp thinkers who love to talk.

How do air signs mix with other elements?

Air + Earth

Air signs have no problem with change. After all, they can go whichever way the wind blows. But it might be hard for these breezy signs to understand the earth signs' fixed ways. Yet, air signs can share a lot. They have a free way of thinking that might just inspire earth signs.

Air + Fire

In nature, air fuels flames. It's no surprise that fire and air are a hot combo. Fire signs are all about action and can help bring air signs' bright ideas to life. Both signs are also outgoing. There is no shortage of fun when these two are together.

Air + Water

Water has big dreams, and air has big plans. By working together, they can make magic. But beware when air and water disagree. A hurricane may suddenly appear in the forecast.

Flying High

The air signs are alike in many ways.
But each sign has traits all its own.

Geminis are playful and carefree.

Libras are caring friends and great listeners.

Aquarians are mega-creative and march to the beat of their own drum.

Keep breezing along to get info on each sign.

If your birthday falls
May 21 through June 20,
your sign is

Gemini

A Sure Sign of Fun

Gemini's **glyph** looks a lot like the Roman numeral two. This glyph makes sense as the Gemini motto might well be "it takes two." Naturally, the body parts ruled by Gemini come in pairs.

Better Look Twice

The symbol for Gemini is twins. This sign isn't two-faced, but Geminis do have two sides to their personality. They can quickly change their moods.

glyph — a symbolic character

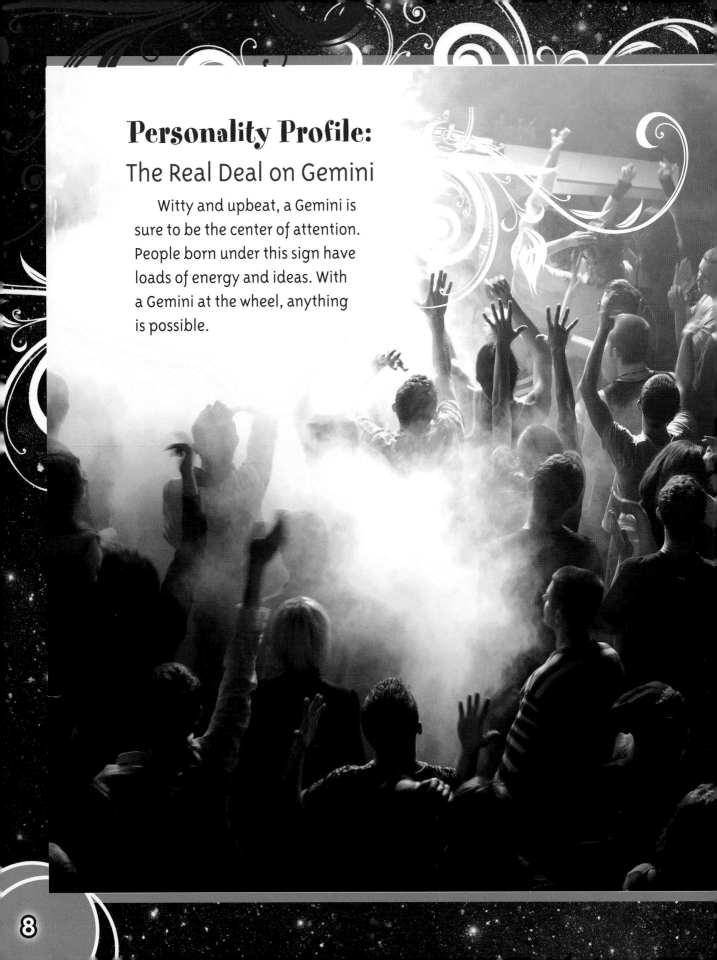

Personality Profile:

The Real Deal on Gemini

Witty and upbeat, a Gemini is sure to be the center of attention. People born under this sign have loads of energy and ideas. With a Gemini at the wheel, anything is possible.

Personality Pluses

clever
curious
full of fun
lively
loves to chat

Personality Minuses

always changes mind
easily bored
gossipy
impatient
nervous

Just the Facts about Gemini

Lucky day of week: Wednesday

Parts of body ruled: hands, arms, shoulders, and lungs

Ruling planet: Mercury

Flower: lily of the valley

Style File

In true star style, Geminis are big on wardrobe changes. They keep their closets stocked with plenty of options. Eye-catching yellow is a sure bet. To top off a glam look, a Gemini may wear a bracelet made with shiny agate. After all, it's a Gemini's lucky stone.

Tapping into Talents

Geminis are born storytellers. They make great journalists and authors. A love for center stage also makes them natural actors and comedians. Event planning is another awesome job. Geminis can be social butterflies that see to all the details.

A Gemini's Social Survival Guide

No doubt about it. Geminis often have tons of friends. But do they get along with everyone? Check out this quick rundown of Gemini friends and foes.

Gemini Friends

A Gemini gets along famously with Libra, Aquarius, and other Geminis. Gemini also matches well with Aries and Leo. These fire signs are very social, seek adventure, and love to laugh.

Gemini Foes

A Gemini just doesn't get a Virgo's need for routine and rules. A Gemini may also clash with Pisces, Taurus, and Capricorn.

The Gemini Cast of Characters

Is Mom or Dad a Gemini?

Chances are your conversations at the dinner table are always lively. Gemini parents are all about sharing knowledge and stories. You can also expect amazing vacations. After all, Geminis love to travel and see the world. Enjoy the ride!

Is Your BFF a Gemini?

Remember that a Gemini's mind is always racing. Try not to take it too hard if your friend's mind wanders during your nightly phone marathons. On the plus side, time flies when you are with this BFF. Keep an open mind. Your friend will always try to talk you into a new adventure. No worries — you're sure to have a great time.

It's All in the Stars:
Famous Geminis

Paula Abdul

Johnny Depp

Anne Frank

Angelina Jolie

Heidi Klum

Marilyn Monroe

Mary-Kate and Ashley Olsen

Natalie Portman

Donald Trump

Venus Williams

Mary-Kate and Ashley Olsen

Birthday: June 13, 1986

Gemini is a natural match for Mary-Kate and Ashley Olsen. After all, this is the sign known for its symbol of twins. One of Hollywood's hottest pairs, they are girls on the go. From designing clothes to acting in movies, there is never a dull moment when these two are around. In true Gemini form, these fashionistas love to travel with a party posse. But who are their best friends? They are each other's BFFs, of course.

If your birthday falls
September 23 through October 22,
your sign is

Libra

A Sign for Justice

The Libra glyph is a setting sun. Some think it looks like an equal sign. Either way makes sense. A sunset shows the meeting of dark and light. The equal sign stands for Libra's need for fairness.

All about Balance

In Roman times, a "libra" was a weight used to balance a pair of scales. So it's no wonder that Libra's symbol is a set of scales. The scales show the sign's sense of balance and fairness.

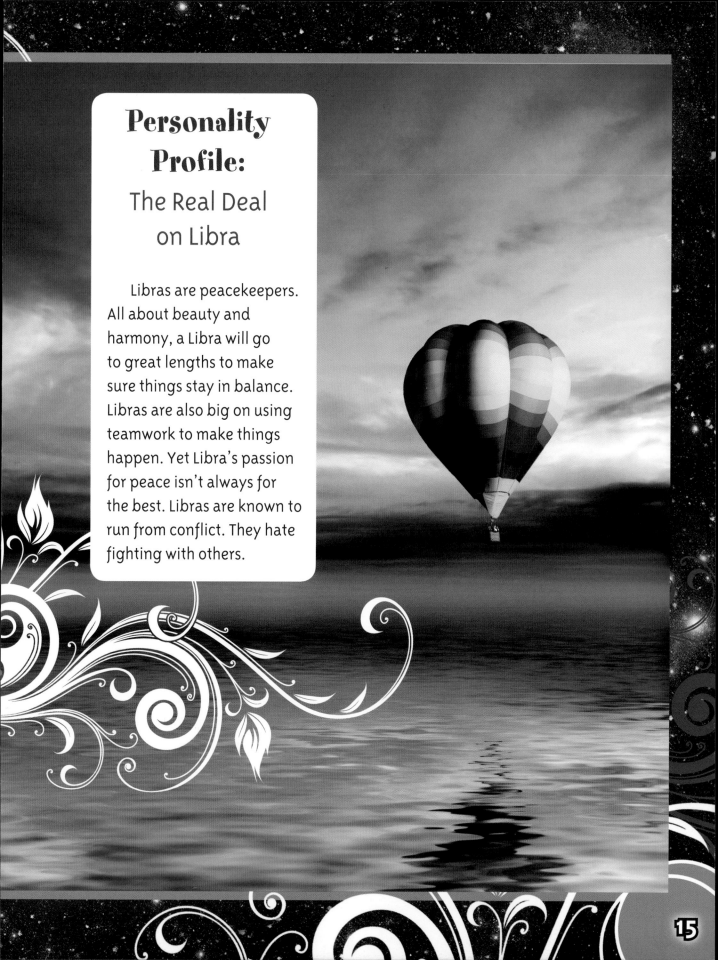

Personality Profile:
The Real Deal on Libra

Libras are peacekeepers. All about beauty and harmony, a Libra will go to great lengths to make sure things stay in balance. Libras are also big on using teamwork to make things happen. Yet Libra's passion for peace isn't always for the best. Libras are known to run from conflict. They hate fighting with others.

Personality Minuses
afraid of conflict
indecisive
insecure
keeps secrets
vain

Personality Pluses
calm
easygoing
fair
polite
trustworthy

Just the Facts about Libra

Parts of body ruled:
lower back area and kidneys

Ruling planet: Venus

Lucky day of week: Friday

Flower: rose

Style File

Polished and put together, Libra's look is all about pieces working in harmony. Libras love classic clothes. But their style is far from boring. Libras are all about the fun. Light blue and lavender are this sign's lucky colors. Opals are a smart pick that will bring a Libra good luck.

The Sky's the Limit

No matter the job, a Libra will get it done. This sign is trustworthy and works well with others. A strong desire for justice may land some Libras careers in law or international relations. Libras might also follow their creative path. People born under this sign make great artists, dancers, and designers.

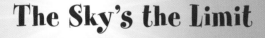

A Libra's Social Survival Guide

Know anyone who seems friendly with everyone? Odds are that he or she is a Libra. A Libra is a great friend to have. This friend can always see both sides and will help smooth out an argument. Which signs are tops on a Libra's list?

Libra Friends

Libra and Aquarius are great matches, but Gemini is top choice. Both Libra and Gemini have a curious nature. They will each seek to learn all there is to know about each other. Leo and Sagittarius can also be fast friends for a Libra.

Libra Foes

Libra may bring out the "crabby" side of Cancer. After all, Cancer is all about deep emotions, and a Libra focuses on deep thoughts. Capricorn is another poor match. This serious and focused sign doesn't understand Libra's need to be social.

The Libra Cast of Characters

Lovestruck by a Libra?

Libras love to be in love. Romantic and attentive, your Libra is sure to be a great catch. Return the favor by giving your crush lots of compliments.

Is Your Teacher a Libra?

No use pouring on the charm. This teacher is sure to treat everyone fairly. Your Libra teacher takes extra care to see that all students get the grade they deserve. Make sure to show your appreciation and give them an "A" for their efforts.

It's All in the Stars:

Famous Libras

Simon Cowell	John Lennon
Matt Damon	John Mayer
Hilary Duff	Eleanor Roosevelt
Zac Efron	Will Smith
Mahatma Gandhi	Serena Williams

Zac Efron

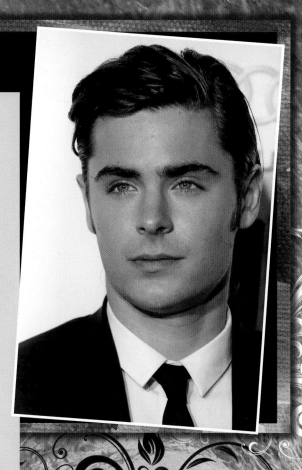

Birthday: October 18, 1987

Acting, singing, sports. Is there anything Zac Efron can't do? This *High School Musical* star is a crush-worthy cutie. And he's also got plenty of talent to spare. Like many Libras, Zac is an achiever both on-screen and off. While attending high school in California, he got great grades. Zac also has that air sign trademark humor. *Bop* magazine's got proof. In an interview, Zac admitted he was a class clown.

If your birthday falls
January 20 through **February 18**,
your sign is

Aquarius

A Powerful Sign

The Aquarius glyph looks like two squiggly lines. These squiggly lines represent waves. Some astrologers say the waves are made of water. Others say they are waves of electricity. In both cases, the glyph shows the extreme power of an Aquarius.

Full of Ideas

Aquarius' symbol is the "Water Bearer." The image for this symbol is sometimes shown as a bucket of water. Like water pouring from a bucket, Aquarians have ideas and wisdom flowing from them.

Personality Profile:
The Real Deal on Aquarius

Meet Aquarius, a rebel with a cause. This sign is fearless and unique. An Aquarius is rarely afraid of what people think. After all, this sign would rather be setting trends than following them. The road less traveled is where you'll find an Aquarius.

Personality Pluses

daring
honest
independent
one of a kind
open-minded

Personality Minuses

acts before thinking
distant
know-it-all
rebel
stubborn

Just the Facts about Aquarius

Parts of body ruled: circulatory system, shins, and ankles

Ruling planet: Uranus

Lucky day of week: Wednesday

Flower: orchid

Style File

Fashion-forward Aquarius loves to be one step ahead of the rest. Looking different is the name of the game. Aquarians might score a fun thrift shop find. Or they might wear their own snazzy creation. Electric blue is their color of choice. For a bit of luck, Aquarians should wear amethyst.

Aquarius at Work

An Aquarius' imagination works nonstop. A person born under this sign could easily invent the next big thing. Both science and engineering are career fields for this brilliant mind. A job on Capitol Hill fits this sign well too.

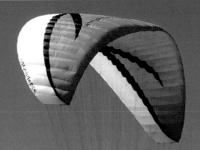

An Aquarius' Social Survival Guide

Aquarians are leaders. They use their smarts and talents for good. When looking for friends, an Aquarius likes people who don't fit in. This sign is also drawn to those who believe in important social causes. Which signs are most likely to join an Aquarius' pack?

Aquarius Friends

The Aquarius clicks well with other air signs. An Aquarius will also find a happy match with Sagittarius. A combo of air and fire is sure to bring adventures.

Aquarius Foes

An Aquarius can't help but tell the truth. This sign's honesty can be too much for a Leo. An Aquarius and Scorpio can be foes too. An Aquarius will raise a red flag when a Scorpio asks for too much time. After all, an Aquarius is a free-floating sign.

Is Your Sibling an Aquarius?

Why does your Aquarius sister disappear into her room for hours? Here's the scoop. Aquarius can be super-social. But this sign needs lots of alone time too. You'll have smooth sailing with your sibling if you can respect her need for peace and quiet.

Crushin' on an Aquarius Hottie?

It can sometimes be hard to read an Aquarius. After all, this sign tends to run hot and cold. Be patient. Once inside an Aquarius' inner circle, you're there to stay. After you've "cracked the code," your Aquarius cutie will want to hear all your deepest thoughts. Don't be afraid to share it all.

It's All in the Stars:
Famous Aquarians

Jennifer Aniston
Judy Blume
Lauren Conrad
Alicia Keys
Abraham Lincoln

Wolfgang Amadeus Mozart
Babe Ruth
Justin Timberlake
John Travolta
Oprah Winfrey

Lauren Conrad

Birthday: February 1, 1986

As MTV's small-screen queen, Lauren Conrad starred in *Laguna Beach* and *The Hills*. For years, Lauren's life was an open book. Today, Lauren is no longer in front of the cameras. But this Aquarius is still living the glam life. Lauren uses her creativity to design clothes and call the shots at fashion shows. She has even written a best-selling book. This Aquarius' star doesn't look like it is going to dim anytime soon.

Quiz: What's Your Style Sign?

Do you love earthy colors? Or are soft fabrics more your style? Take this quiz to find out if the stars rule your sense of fashion.

1. Time to get ready for school. How do you decide what to wear?

Ⓐ I'm all about comfort to get through the day.
Ⓑ It all depends on my mood. If I'm feeling blue, I dress the part.
Ⓒ Eeney, meeney, miney, mo: I go for whatever pops out.
Ⓓ I pick whatever will get me noticed walking down the hallway.

2. What's your style bible?

Ⓐ *Seventeen*
Ⓑ *Girls' Life*
Ⓒ *Etsy.com*
Ⓓ *Teen Vogue*

3. Which of these phrases describes your look?

Ⓐ Tastefully simple
Ⓑ Girly girl
Ⓒ True original
Ⓓ Label queen

4. If you could ditch your gym class uniform, you'd wear:

Ⓐ a fun Polo shirt and khaki shorts.
Ⓑ a flowing sundress with leggings.
Ⓒ I'd rather ditch gym class, period.
Ⓓ a bright-red tracksuit with bling.

5. What's your favorite color?

Ⓐ Navy
Ⓑ Green
Ⓒ Purple
Ⓓ Gold

6. Pick your celeb style idol:

Ⓐ Audrey Hepburn
Ⓑ Anne Hathaway
Ⓒ Gwen Stefani
Ⓓ Jennifer Lopez

7. What one word describes what you look for in clothes?

Ⓐ Function
Ⓑ Comfort
Ⓒ Flair
Ⓓ Glamour

8. Time to go jewelry shopping! What catches your eye?

Ⓐ Diamond stud earrings
Ⓑ A long skeleton key necklace
Ⓒ Brightly colored bangles
Ⓓ A bejeweled tiara

9. It's time for a new haircut. What will your next look be?

Ⓐ Pretty much the same look you always sport. Hey, if it works, it works.
Ⓑ Something unique. You don't want to look like everyone else.
Ⓒ Something super-cute that's so trendy.
Ⓓ Long and soft. Either the cut or the color will be an attention grabber.

10. What type of shoes do your feet fancy?

Ⓐ Well-worn tennis shoes
Ⓑ Comfy sandals
Ⓒ Sequined high tops
Ⓓ Heels with an animal print

Zodiac Chart

Aries
March 21–April 19
Fire

- brave
- confident
- energetic

Leo
July 23–August 22
Fire

- dignified
- generous
- playful

Sagittarius
November 22–December 21
Fire

- adventurous
- cheerful
- fun

Taurus
April 20–May 20
Earth

- friendly
- loyal
- trustworthy

Virgo
August 23–September 22
Earth

- helpful
- observant
- practical

Capricorn
December 22–January 19
Earth

- determined
- hardworking
- wise

Gemini
May 21–June 20
Air

- clever
- curious
- lively

Libra
September 23–October 22
Air

- charming
- fair
- polite

Aquarius
January 20–February 18
Air

- daring
- honest
- independent

Cancer
June 21–July 22
Water

- caring
- gentle
- sensitive

Scorpio
October 23–November 21
Water

- confident
- fearless
- flirty

Pisces
February 19–March 20
Water

- artistic
- creative
- kind

Quiz Key

When scoring your answers, **A** equals 1 point, **B** equals 2 points, **C** equals 3 points, and **D** equals 4 points. Add them up to discover which element is the best style match for you!

35–40 = Your clothes are all about sizzle. No doubt about it, your glam style has **fire** signs written all over it.

26–34 = You'll breeze in and out of a mall. And your shopping bags will say **air** signs all the way.

16–25 = You think creative and flowing is the only way to go. Don't be surprised if you're swept away by the **water** signs' style.

10–15 = Your clothes simply rock. It's plain to see, **earth** signs rule your closet.

Glossary

astrology (uh-STROL-uh-jee) — the study of how the positions of stars and planets affect people's lives

destiny (DESS-tuh-nee) — your fate or future events in your life

element (EL-uh-muhnt) — one of the four categories of signs found in the zodiac; the elements are air, earth, fire, and water.

glyph (GLIF) — a symbolic character; each of the 12 astrology signs has individual glyphs.

horoscope (HOR-uh-skope) — a reading of the position of the stars and planets and how they might affect a person's life

predict (pri-DIKT) — to say what you think will happen in the future

trait (TRATE) — a quality or characteristic that makes one person different from another

unique (yoo-NEEK) — one of a kind

zodiac (ZOH-dee-ak) — the arrangement of signs that fill a year, beginning and ending in March

Read More

Aslan, Madalyn. *What's Your Sign? A Cosmic Guide for Young Astrologers.* New York: Grosset & Dunlap, 2002.

Asselin, Kristine Carlson. *Taurus, Virgo, and Capricorn: All about the Earth Signs.* Zodiac Fun. Mankato, Minn.: Capstone Press, 2010.

Jones, Jen. *Fashion.* 10 Things You Need to Know About. Mankato, Minn.: Capstone Press, 2008.

Internet Sites

FactHound offers a safe, fun way to find Internet sites related to this book. All of the sites on FactHound have been researched by our staff.

Here's all you do:

Visit *www.facthound.com*

FactHound will fetch the best sites for you!

Index

About the Author

A Los Angeles-based author, **Jen Jones** has written more than 35 books for Capstone Press. (Born on August 3rd, she's a proud Leo lioness!) Along with writing books, Jen has published stories in magazines such as *American Cheerleader*, *Dance Spirit*, *Ohio Today*, and *Pilates Style*. In the past, she was a staff writer for *E! Online* and *PBS Kids*, as well as a Web site producer for major talk shows such as *The Jenny Jones Show*, *The Sharon Osbourne Show*, and *The Larry Elder Show*. Jen is also a member of the Society of Children's Book Writers and Illustrators.